W9-BZY-161

JUL _ - 2012

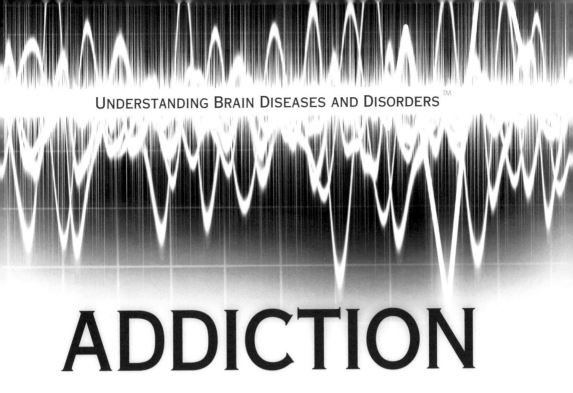

UNDERSTANDING BRAIN DISEASES AND DISORDERS™

ADDICTION

BARBARA GOTTFRIED HOLLANDER

ROSEN
PUBLISHING®

New York

Published in 2012 by The Rosen Publishing Group, Inc.
29 East 21st Street, New York, NY 10010

Library of Congress Cataloging-in-Publication Data

Hollander, Barbara, 1970–
Addiction/Barbara Gottfried Hollander.—1st ed.
    p. cm.—(Understanding brain diseases and disorders)
Includes bibliographical references and index.
ISBN 978-1-4488-5540-7 (library binding)
1. Compulsive behavior—Social aspects. 2. Addicts—Psychology. 3.
Substance abuse—Treatment. I. Title.
RC533.H653 2012
616.86—dc23

                                                                2011014227

Manufactured in China

CPSIA Compliance Information: Batch #W12YA: For further information, contact Rosen Publishing, New York, New York, at
1-800-237-9932.

CONTENTS

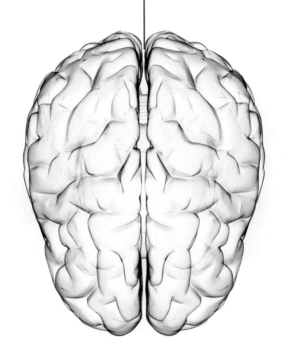

Introduction

In January 2011, a man named Ted Williams became an overnight sensation as the "man with the golden voice." For over ten years, Williams was homeless, living on the street and begging for money. Then one day, someone posted a video of Williams on the video-sharing Web site YouTube, and it changed his life. Businesses such as Kraft Macaroni & Cheese and the Cleveland Cavaliers responded to his deep, rich voice with job offers to work as their spokesperson. Williams appeared on shows such as *The Early Show*, *The Today Show*, and *Late Night with Jimmy Fallon*.

Then, things started to fall apart for Williams. The man with a golden voice had been struggling with alcohol and drug addiction for fifteen years. These addictions had caused him to trade his original dream of being a radio announcer for living on the streets of Ohio. Addiction also threatened his second chance at professional success. Shortly after the YouTube video aired, Williams admitted that he was drinking a lot and agreed to undergo treatment.

Williams is an addict. He is one of millions of Americans who suffer from a chronic but treatable brain disorder known as addiction. Addiction involves a loss of control and the repeated use of a drug or activity. The disorder changes the structure and processing abilities of the brain and distorts the way that the brain interprets and communicates signals. Substance addiction and abuse can also cause brain damage and death.

Recovering addicts are people who no longer want to engage in drug abuse or an addictive activity (such as gambling). As with other diseases, addiction needs to be treated and managed each day. Ongoing medical research is changing the way addiction is viewed and is exploring the biological factors that make people more prone to addiction. These developments increase the chances for recovering addicts to lead sober and productive lives.

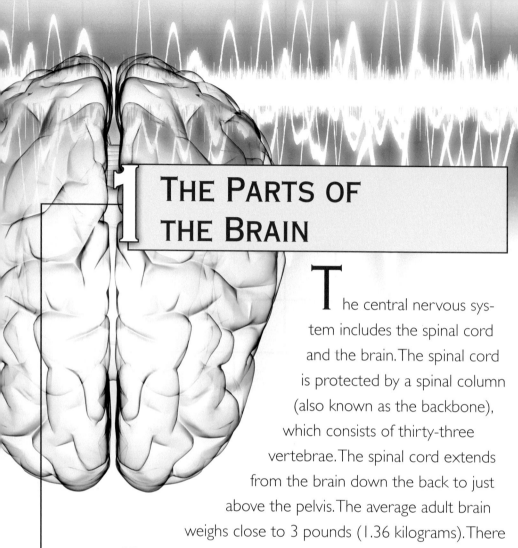

1 THE PARTS OF THE BRAIN

The central nervous system includes the spinal cord and the brain. The spinal cord is protected by a spinal column (also known as the backbone), which consists of thirty-three vertebrae. The spinal cord extends from the brain down the back to just above the pelvis. The average adult brain weighs close to 3 pounds (1.36 kilograms). There are different parts of the brain, including the cerebrum, cerebellum, limbic system, and the brain stem.

The Cerebrum

The cerebrum is the largest part of the brain, making up 85 percent of the brain's weight. Also known as the cerebral cortex, the cerebrum is the thinking part of the brain. Its wrinkled structure helps the brain function more efficiently because it increases the surface area. When a brain has more surface area, it has more places for cells called neurons. These special cells help people process information.

The cerebrum has two sides, or hemispheres: the right hemisphere and the left hemisphere. In general, the right side of the brain controls the left side of a person's body, while the left side of the brain controls the right side of a person's body. According to many scientists, the left side is responsible for math, logic, and speech. The right side focuses on creativity, such as music and art. The right and left hemispheres are attached by a part of the brain called the corpus callosum.

The Cerebellum

The cerebellum is the second largest part of the brain. It is only one-eighth the size of the cerebrum. Located in the back of the brain, the cerebellum controls movement, balance, and equilibrium. The cerebellum focuses on the timing of movements. For example, it allows a person to type the letters on a keyboard in the right order, like pushing "t," "h," "e" to spell the word "the." The cerebellum also helps with balance and equilibrium. Equilibrium is a state where forces cancel each other out so that things remain the same. For example, a person riding a bike may shift her weight to the right if she begins to fall to the left. This action cancels out the feeling of falling to the left and allows the bike rider to remain balanced.

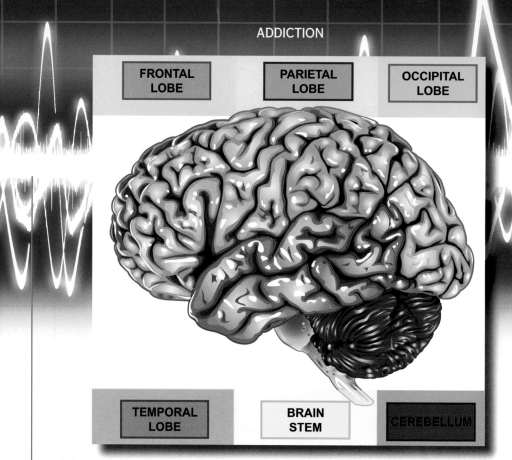

| FRONTAL LOBE | PARIETAL LOBE | OCCIPITAL LOBE |

| TEMPORAL LOBE | BRAIN STEM | CEREBELLUM |

The frontal lobe helps people speak, move, feel, plan activities, and control their behavior. The parietal lobe focuses on sensory information and spatial relationships. The occipital lobe allows people to process what they see, like colors and shapes. The temporal lobe aids in understanding what people hear, see, say, and remember.

The Limbic System

Located under the cerebrum, the limbic system is responsible for emotion and memories. Many emotions come from the limbic system, like feeling sad or happy. This system includes several parts, such as the amygdala, the hippocampus, and the hypothalamus. Shaped like an almond, the amygdala is located in the medial temporal lobe. It responds to things that induce emotions, such as pleasure, anger, aggression, and fear. The hippocampus is shaped like a small sea horse and allows a person to turn short-term memories into long-term ones. For example, a college student who remembers his first-grade teacher is using his hippocampus.

The hypothalamus is responsible for homeostasis, or maintaining equilibrium. Think of homeostasis as setting a thermostat, which maintains the temperature in a room. If the room becomes too hot, the air-conditioning comes on and brings the room back to a set temperature. Now, think about the importance of maintaining a certain level of functioning each day. If a person becomes hungry, the process of homeostasis encourages eating. The hypothalamus also regulates being thirsty, feeling pain or pleasure, being angry or aggressive, and being sexually satisfied. It even regulates a person's body temperature (just like the thermostat) and sends out signals to sweat or to shiver in response to being hot or cold. The hypothalamus receives input from other parts of the body and then responds using the autonomic nervous system and pituitary gland (which makes and releases hormones).

The Brain Stem

All information that travels between the brain and other parts of the body goes through the brain stem. This part of the brain is responsible for breathing, digestion, heart rate, and blood pressure—all of the things a person needs to stay alive. The brain stem connects the brain to the spinal cord and focuses on involuntary actions. Involuntary actions are ones that are performed automatically, or without thinking. For example, the brain stem signals the heart to pump more blood when a person exercises.

Bones surround both parts of the central nervous system. Bones in the skull protect the brain, while the vertebrae protect the spinal cord.

The Peripheral Nervous System

The peripheral nervous system consists of groups of neurons that extend to muscles, organs, and throughout the whole body. Neurons are single nerve cells. Nerves carry signals and messages to different parts of the body. The brain interprets these messages, makes decisions, and then sends out signals to the rest of the body through the nerves. Nerves control both voluntary and involuntary actions and allow the rest of the body to respond to the brain's orders.

Neurotransmitters: Dopamine and GABA

Neurotransmitters perform many important jobs in a person's body. They speak and listen to a body's needs and wants. Dopamine is one type of neurotransmitter. Dopamine is known as the "pleasure pathway" because it is responsible for making people feel the emotion of pleasure. Dopamine processes and sends information to the brain about feeling good. It is linked to cravings because people often associate cravings with pleasure. This neurotransmitter is also involved with rewards and motivation. It allows people to see the benefits of certain actions and motivates them to act toward getting those rewards.

GABA (gamma-aminobutyric acid) is another kind of neurotransmitter. It is an inhibitory neurotransmitter, which means that it keeps the brain from getting too excited. GABA (technically an amino acid) is associated with calmness, relaxation, and sleep. GABA is the inhibitory neurotransmitter found most in a person's body. Besides calming the brain, GABA affects movement control and vision. People suffering from anxiety, depression, and alcoholism often have low levels of GABA.

Nerve cells use neurotransmitters to tell each other what to do. Neurotransmitters are chemical communicators. Suppose you have an itch on your arm. A cell in your arm may send out a neurotransmitter to another cell with a message. The neurotransmitter in your arm travels with this information

Nerves communicate both electrically and chemically. Chemically, neurons transmit information to other neurons across synapses, or meeting places where nerve impulses travel from an axon terminal to a neuron.

to an area called a receptor. The receptor is located in another cell. The neurotransmitter from the first cell fits into the receptor of the second cell, like a key fits into a lock. Once in place, the neurotransmitter makes the second cell realize what it needs to do—scratch.

Scratching is an example of one action. Now, think about how many actions a body does in a day, an hour, a minute, or even each second (including breathing, eating, and speaking). In order for these actions to occur, there has to be the right amount and kind of neurotransmitters and their receptor sites.

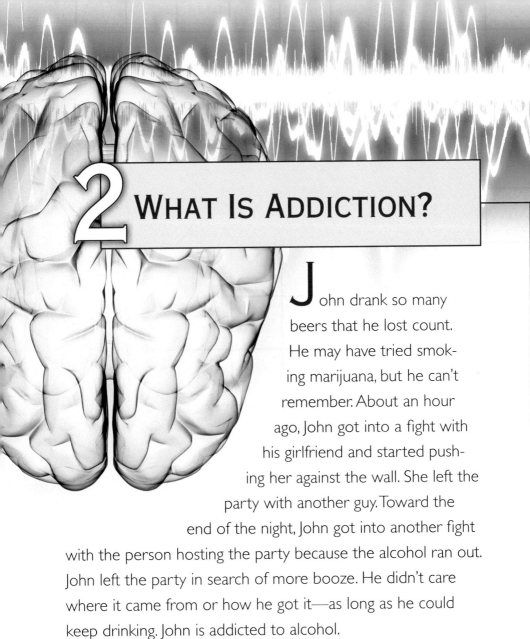

2 WHAT IS ADDICTION?

John drank so many beers that he lost count. He may have tried smoking marijuana, but he can't remember. About an hour ago, John got into a fight with his girlfriend and started pushing her against the wall. She left the party with another guy. Toward the end of the night, John got into another fight with the person hosting the party because the alcohol ran out. John left the party in search of more booze. He didn't care where it came from or how he got it—as long as he could keep drinking. John is addicted to alcohol.

Substance Addiction

Addiction is a chronic, but treatable, brain disease that involves a loss of control. It results from changes to the brain that cause people to alter their behaviors. Doctors can see these changes on brain imaging tests, which indicate that addiction damages parts of the brain, specifically the cerebrum and the limbic system. These parts of the brain affect decision making, learning, memory, and behavioral control.

In the example above, John is suffering from substance addiction, or a loss of control over the need for alcohol and other drugs. Substance addiction is measured by (1) if a person needs more of the drug to feel the same effects over time (building up "tolerance") and (2) if a person suffers withdrawal as the drug leaves the body. People with substance addiction use different kinds of drugs, including nicotine, alcohol, marijuana, pharmaceutical sedatives and barbiturates, stimulants, ecstasy, and heroin.

Nicotine

Nicotine is found in cigarettes and other kinds of tobacco products. According to the Surgeon General's report, addiction to tobacco products is similar to other

Making cigarettes begins when tobacco leaves and stems are grown, dried, and cured. Broken leaves are then combined with paper pulp, ammonia, sugar, and carcinogens (which can cause cancer).

drug addictions, such as heroin and cocaine. Nicotine increases the carbon monoxide levels in the blood, which lowers the amount of oxygen that flows to the brain, heart, and other organs. Specifically, nicotine affects the right hemisphere of the brain.

Nicotine also increases the stress hormone known as cortisol. Over time, increased cortisol levels can decrease cognitive (or thinking) abilities, decrease muscle tone and bone density, lower the ability to process glucose (or sugar), increase blood pressure, and make it easier to get sick (by lowering the immune system). Nicotine addiction puts people at higher risks for asthma, heart disease, heart attack, and pneumonia. Smoking or consuming nicotine-containing tobacco products also increases the risk for several kinds of cancer, including lung, cervical, head and neck, and brain cancers.

Alcohol

Alcohol is a type of drug known as a depressant, which reduces the flow of brain signals. It destroys brain cells, mostly in the left hemisphere, which is the site of language and logic. The number of destroyed cells depends on various factors, such as the amount of alcohol consumed and a person's body weight.

Alcohol specifically affects the dopamine, serotonin, and GABA neurotransmitters. It decreases communication and can lead to confusion, memory loss, blackouts, and uncoordinated movements. Alcohol addiction can also result in a coma and respiratory (breathing) failure.

Alcohol addiction is the third-leading cause of death in the United States, behind heart disease and cancer. It is as addictive as cocaine.

Marijuana

Known by over two hundred names (such as pot, weed, and grass), marijuana is a combination of parts of the hemp plant. Its main chemical, called tetrahydrocannabinol (THC), releases dopamine in the brain. This creates the pleasure effect of feeling high. But repeated use of marijuana and other drugs to achieve a high damages the dopamine system. This damage may result in lower dopamine levels, receptors that no longer work, or smaller cells with D2 receptor sites. Brain-imaging tests (such as PET scans) confirm that people addicted to drugs, like marijuana, have low activity in the median forebrain bundle. This bundle is full of D2 dopamine receptors.

Pharmaceutical Sedatives and Barbiturates

Pharmaceutical sedatives and barbiturates are depressants. Doctors prescribe them to help people who have sleep problems and anxiety (or high levels of nervousness). They depress brain activity by enhancing the GABA neurotransmitter system and making people feel even more relaxed and sleepy. Doctors usually recommend that people take them for five to seven days. Unfortunately, many people become addicted to these drugs (which include Valium, BuSpar, and Klonopin) because their effects only last for a short period of time and require higher quantities to produce the same effect over time. While allowing people to feel relaxed, pharmaceutical sedatives can also cause memory problems, slurred speech, confusion, inability to drive safely, and decreased peripheral visual awareness when used in excess.

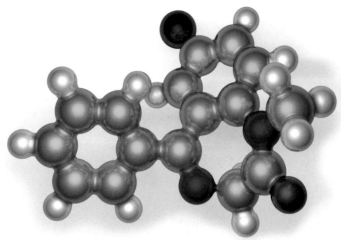

Pharmaceutical sedatives such as diazepam (Valium), the molecular model of which is displayed here, are often highly addictive and should only be taken under a doctor's supervision.

Stimulants

Stimulants produce the opposite effects of depressants. Stimulants speed up activity, particularly heart rate, breathing, blood pressure, and eye pupil activity. This causes intense alertness and physical activity. Stimulants also decrease appetite, so people have used them for weight loss.

Stimulants can be taken in different ways, such as swallowed, injected, snorted, or smoked. Cocaine is a kind of stimulant and is the fourth most addictive drug. It tightens the blood vessels in the brain, which results in lower brain functions. Like marijuana, cocaine also damages the dopamine delivery system. Long-term effects of addiction to stimulants include heart disease, heart attacks, breathing failure, strokes, seizures, blurred vision, coma, hallucinations, psychosis (being out of control), and death.

Ecstasy and Heroin

Ecstasy is an entactogen drug. This group of drugs was first produced to help people overcome traumatic experiences by improving their moods. But use of these drugs also results in being confused, anxious, disoriented, scared, and out of control. Entactogens disturb the senses and distort sensitivity to music and color. Ecstasy takes serotonin out of the brain, which can take weeks for the brain to replace. Serotonin is a neurotransmitter that affects mood, appetite, the senses, and risk preferences.

Heroin is the third most addictive drug. Heroin comes from the opium (poppy) plant and can be snorted, sniffed, injected, or smoked. Injecting the drug puts it directly into the bloodstream. People who snort heroin also absorb the drug into their bloodstream very quickly through their nasal passages. Heroin enters the brain, undergoes chemical changes to become morphine, and binds to opioid receptors. These receptors are linked to feelings of pain and pleasure. Heroin addiction damages the nervous, respiratory, and cardiovascular systems. It also decreases liver function.

The juice of the poppy leaf is used to make opium (found in morphine, heroin, and codeine). India and the Golden Triangle (borders of Burma, Thailand, and Laos) are the two main opium-producing regions.

Behavioral Addictions

A behavioral addiction involves uncontrollable acts that dominate a person's time and attention. They disrupt a person's life and can have significant social, financial, and health costs. As with substance addiction, behavioral addicts often choose activities that, at least initially, elicit excitement and pleasure. They continue to crave this pleasure, despite destructive effects both to themselves and those around them.

19

Gambling and Sex Addiction

Gambling involves betting valuable items (like money) on uncertain outcomes. It is a risky venture, which creates a stimulant response (such as increased heart beat, blood pressure, and breathing). People gamble because they enjoy the thrill or to escape their daily lives, despite serious consequences. For example, many gambling addicts will do just about anything to obtain money, such as using up all of their family's savings.

Sex addiction involves several steps that begin with constant sex-related thoughts, followed by engaging in a group of sexual rituals (such as looking at pornography). Finally, a sex addict has sex, sometimes with multiple partners, regardless of the consequences, such as health risks. Sex dominates a sex addict's life, produces a high (since it releases dopamine), and requires more of the act to produce the same feeling over time. Sex addiction often involves deviant sexual behavior (or acts that are far from normal sexual acts). This addiction is about the physical aspects of sex and has nothing to do with the emotional aspects of making love.

Food and Computer Addiction

A food addiction occurs when a person uses food and eating behaviors as coping mechanisms. According to Kathie Mattison, a registered dietician with Eating Experts, people are "'addicted' to eating behaviors, which disrupt normal relationships between food and the body." For example, binge eating disorder consists of consuming large amounts of food (even after feeling full), without anything to balance this action (such as a lot of exercise).

Anorexia is another eating disorder, where people severely and dangerously limit food intake or overexercise. The American Academy of Child & Adolescent Psychiatry reports that up to ten out of one hundred young American women suffer from eating disorders, although such disorders can affect young men as well.

Bulimia is another kind of eating disorder and involves a cycle of binge eating and purging. Vomiting, taking laxatives, and excessive exercising are purging activities.

Computer addiction is a recent and controversial issue. It is also called Internet addiction, online addiction, and even Internet addiction disorder (IAD). There is a compulsive part, but also a destructive, antisocial component. Computer addicts live in worlds that exist on the computer and neglect the real world, including their family, home, and work. The most popular forms of computer addiction are cybersex addiction, cyber-relationship addiction, online gambling, information overload, and computer games.

What the Tests Show

There are brain imaging tests that show how the brain functions and even allow doctors to view brain damage and repair in action. These tests include the MRI (magnetic resonance imaging), DTI (diffusion tensor imaging), and PET (positron emission tomography). Imaging tests have changed some of the views and treatments of substance addiction.

Years ago, people believed that addiction was a personality problem or a moral weakness. Today, addiction is known as a disease, which substitutes a person's regular needs and activities with those that help the addict continue abusing a substance or activity. Substance addiction involves brain damage that can be seen and measured on imaging tests. For example, a test from the brain of an alcoholic may show the shrinkage of a once normal, healthy brain (mainly in the cerebrum). This occurs because alcohol destroys brain cells.

Researchers have also discovered that the brain repairs itself. It may take years for the brain to return to its pre-drug abuse state, but repair is possible for many addicts. This repair depends on different factors, including the kinds of drugs abused, how long the drugs were taken, and a person's genes. But, in general, a person who is sober (drug-free) for at least six to ten months should undergo significant brain repair.

Work and Shopping Addiction

Work addiction refers to people who work compulsively and excessively. The American Psychiatric Association does not recognize this kind of behavior as a true addiction because it does not meet the clinical definition. However, some medical experts still address the symptoms and prescribe treatments for this behavior. For instance, work addicts may find that work negatively impacts their social lives. They may also feel helpless over setting limits and suffer physically from their decisions.

According to a December 2006 *Psychiatric Times* survey, shopping addiction affects almost 6 percent of Americans. This kind of addiction involves compulsive shopping (or feeling a strong urge to shop). As with work addiction, there is disagreement about whether this kind of behavior is an actual addiction. However, shopping addiction does share certain traits with other addictions. Specifically, shopping addicts spend a lot of time and money on the addiction. They shop compulsively and excessively, regardless of financial and social costs. Shopping addicts also report feelings of pleasure when making purchases and suffer from withdrawal when not engaging in the act.

Biological Risk Factors for Addiction

There are certain factors that put people at risk for addiction. Family history affects a person's chances of becoming an addict. For example, according to the HBO documentary *Addiction*, more

than 60 percent of alcoholics come from families with alcoholics. Age and gender also affect risk. *Addiction* reports that 40 percent of people who begin drinking before the age of fifteen will become alcoholics. In general, younger people are more likely to become addicted to drugs than older people. Men are also more likely than women to become addicted to drugs and gambling. Once addicted, though, women may become more severely addicted.

Addiction to alcohol is believed to be related to family history. Alcoholism can be passed down from generation to generation.

Recently, medical researchers have looked at the stress diathesis model of addiction. This type of model states that biological factors may cause certain people to be more prone to developing addictions. A person who is more prone to addictions may not develop the addiction. Or this person may be affected by one or more stressors and actually develop the addiction. A stressor is something that causes stress by disrupting homeostasis, or maintaining equilibrium.

How a person reacts to a stressor depends on biological factors. Biological factors include a person's genes, brain functions, and responses to stress. According to one 2010 study by M. A. Enoch and others in *Biological Psychiatry*, people have genes and codes for GABA receptor subtypes. A certain GABRA2 genotype combined with too much stress as a child increases the risk for addiction. Childhood traumas, including neglect and sexual abuse, increase the risk for addiction.

Social Risk Factors for Addiction

Many addicts, especially alcoholics, begin using as teens. These teens may experiment with different drugs, wanting to see what it feels like to get high just once. But the frontal lobe of the brain that controls impulses is not yet developed in teens. So they are less equipped to make choices involving risky behaviors and to stop before they lose control. Teens are also subject to peer pressure. For example, a teen may go to a party and start drinking because all of his friends are doing it. Even though he may feel uncomfortable at first, this teen may end up abusing alcohol.

Lastly, the media publicize the drug addictions of celebrities, like famous actors, actresses, and athletes. Some people (particularly teens) may view these stars as role models and feel that taking drugs is acceptable because famous people do it. The cerebrum is responsible for helping people make good decisions and limit risky behavior. It is also the part of the brain that would help teens realize that the drug addictions of people, even famous people, are mental illnesses that can result in death.

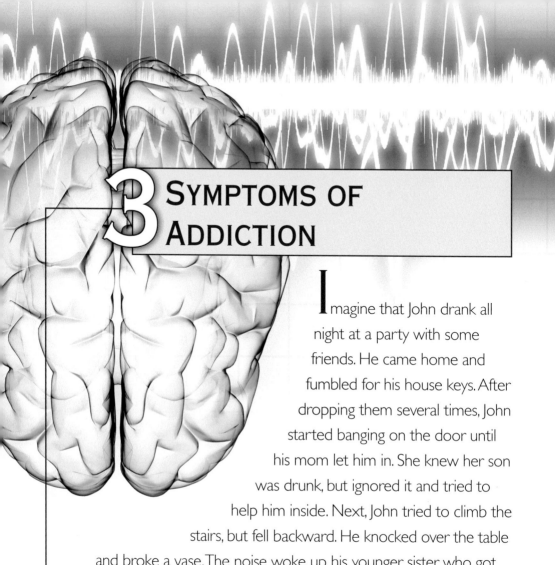

3 SYMPTOMS OF ADDICTION

Imagine that John drank all night at a party with some friends. He came home and fumbled for his house keys. After dropping them several times, John started banging on the door until his mom let him in. She knew her son was drunk, but ignored it and tried to help him inside. Next, John tried to climb the stairs, but fell backward. He knocked over the table and broke a vase. The noise woke up his younger sister, who got out of bed and was standing at the top of the stairs, watching her drunk brother stumble to get up. Their mother stood next to him, as if watching a movie that would repeat itself the following night.

Psychological Symptoms

Many teens like John start drinking by experimenting. Experimentation involves trying something new. Drug

Stealing to support one's addiction is a clear sign that there is a problem. Addicts often resort to theft when they no longer have the financial means to feed their habit.

experimentation includes trying out alcohol, marijuana, nicotine (by smoking a cigarette), or another drug. Teens experiment for different reasons, like peer pressure or wanting to know what it feels like to get high. Often when a person tries a drug once, he or she continues to take the drug. So, what begins as experimentation can end in addiction.

Addictions are accompanied by cravings, or strong desires. Addicts crave a particular substance or activity. They are driven by the impulse to obtain and use these items. Addicts are

Distorted Thought Processes

An addict, who is unwilling to admit an addiction, may provide rationalizations for his or her behavior. In psychiatry, rationalizing is explaining a person's actions in a way that makes sense, while hiding the motivation behind these actions. For example, suppose that John steals his sister's allowance money to buy beer. When his mother confronts him about it, John explains that he needed the money to help out a friend who is throwing a party. Rather than admit his addiction, John diverts the focus to helping out his friend. By rationalizing his action, John does not take responsibility for having an addiction, stealing from his sister, or the damage that was done to his family relationships (such as loss of trust and respect).

Because drugs change the parts of the brain responsible for thinking and reacting, many addicts have distorted thought processes. They view situations as all or nothing, such as, "If I do not buy the drug now, I will never have it." They focus on instant gratification, not thinking about the long-term effects of their actions. In the scenario above, John was only concerned with getting money to buy alcohol today. He did not see the long-term effects on himself or others. Addicts may also feel personally ineffective, which means that they doubt their own capability. This makes addicts feel powerless over their addictions and less willing to seek help.

preoccupied, compulsive, and even obsessed with the objects of their addictions. For example, a drug addict may spend hours every day thinking about how to obtain money to buy a drug and where the drug can be bought. People addicted to drugs are fueled by the satisfaction that they initially receive from indulging their addictions. Eventually, changes in the brain, particularly in the cerebrum and limbic systems, cause an addictive person to use a drug—at any cost, including ruining relationships and death.

Addictions are about a loss of control. Addicts have a sense of desperation, or urgent need, for a substance or activity. They feel that they cannot live without them because they have become dependent on these drugs or activities. This dependence causes addicts to eventually withdraw from healthy everyday routines. For example, an alcoholic may no longer be interested in going to school or spending time with family. Instead, he or she may focus on ways to obtain money for more alcohol or try to make new friends who will provide this alcohol. Addicts also move away from healthy relationship dynamics. Instead of treating a person with respect, a drug addict may view a person as a means to satisfy his or her addiction.

Physical Symptoms

Substance addictions cause changes in the brain, specifically to the cerebrum and the limbic system. The cerebrum is responsible for impulse control, or the ability to control the desire to be satisfied immediately. Imagine that a young person attends a party and sees some friends smoking marijuana. Impulse

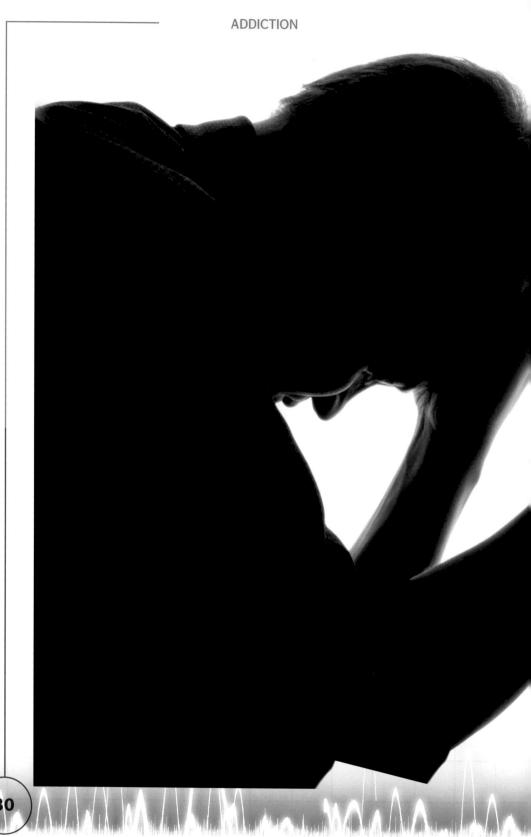

control allows the person to think before acting. It can stop a person from engaging in risky actions, such as trying drugs for the first time. But without impulse control, the person may just react to his friends by smoking the marijuana, too. Both the frontal and parietal lobes of the cerebrum also play a role in cravings, or strong desires to consume something. For example, the parietal lobe causes a person to react to a craving for alcohol, while the frontal lobe is responsible for controlling the impulse to drink as much alcohol as possible.

As already discussed, neurotrans-mitters are chemical communicators. They can stimulate (speed up) or inhibit (slow down) the brain. Substance addiction affects neurotransmitters and changes the ways that nerve cells send, receive, and process informa-tion. For example, the chemical structures of marijuana and heroin

According to the National Center for Biotechnology Information, men who consume at least fifteen drinks a week and women who con-sume at least twelve drinks a week are at risk for becoming alcoholics.

Alcohol-related behaviors include withdrawing from normal activities (like school or work), which can lead to depression.

imitate natural neurotransmitters. These drugs can lock into nerve cell receptors, activate them, and send out the wrong brain signals.

Damage to the neurotransmitters can actually cause an addict's brain to think that drug dependency is necessary and desirable to function normally. For example, alcohol releases more dopamine and serotonin into the body, which makes an alcoholic think that drinking is fun and encourages more drinking. In general, substances of abuse involve the limbic system because they affect the brain's reward circuit. This circuit releases neurotransmitters like dopamine, which creates a rush of "feeling good." When nerve cells and brain functions adapt to drug addictions, it is called neuroadaptation.

As the brain adapts to its new addictive state, substance abusers develop tolerances. According to the National Institute on Alcohol Abuse and Alcoholism, alcoholics display functional tolerance when they display fewer outward effects of being drunk—even with high blood alcohol concentrations (BACs). This means that over time, alcoholics need more alcohol to achieve the same effects (or high). People develop tolerances to different activities at different rates. Environments can also affect tolerance, like developing a higher tolerance when abusing a substance in the same setting each time.

Withdrawal

Addicts experience withdrawal when they stop using drugs or engaging in other kinds of addictions. Physical and mental symptoms of withdrawal include anxiety, insomnia (not sleeping), seizures, and hallucinations (like seeing something that is not really there). Periods of withdrawal depend on the substance or activity. For example, a person with an alcohol addiction typically experiences three to five days of withdrawal, while withdrawal symptoms can last one to two days following a two- to three-day cocaine binge.

Many withdrawal symptoms for drugs are the opposite of the drugs' effects. For example, alcohol makes people feel drowsy because it binds to GABA receptors and decreases glutamate. But the symptoms from alcohol withdrawal include agitation, anxiety, increased heart rate and blood pressure, and even seizures. So, an alcohol addiction depresses the central nervous system, but withdrawing from alcohol stimulates the central nervous system. Because some of the symptoms from substance withdrawal can be life threatening, many addicts undergo detoxification (detox) in medical facilities or other safe environments.

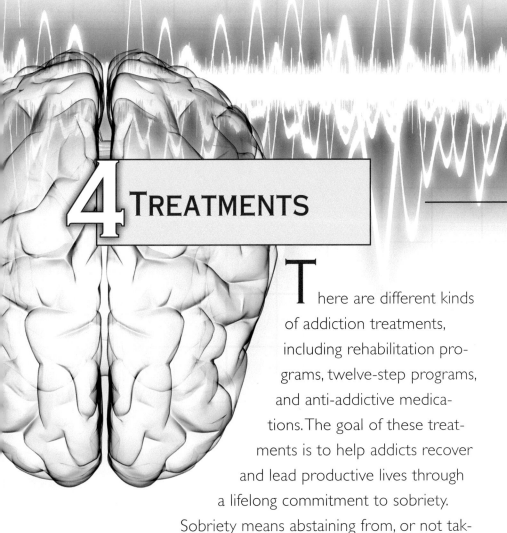

4 TREATMENTS

There are different kinds of addiction treatments, including rehabilitation programs, twelve-step programs, and anti-addictive medications. The goal of these treatments is to help addicts recover and lead productive lives through a lifelong commitment to sobriety. Sobriety means abstaining from, or not taking, drugs. Recovering addicts may choose to do one, some, or all of the treatments.

Treatment Programs

Some recovering addicts seek outpatient treatment programs. Outpatient programs allow the person to live at home, while acquiring the tools necessary for a life of sobriety. This kind of treatment consists of therapy, such as group therapy, individual

Recovery programs, such as the one shown here, can help addicts learn the skills necessary to maintain sobriety.

therapy, or psychopharmacological therapy (which includes medications). Therapy involves discussing painful experiences, taking responsibility for one's actions, realizing the importance of making healthy choices, and developing coping mechanisms.

Cognitive behavioral therapy is one type of therapy used to treat addiction. It is based on the idea that a person's feelings and behavior are caused by thoughts—not by external stimuli, like people or events. If recovering addicts can change their thoughts, they can also change their behavior, even if their environments remain the same. In the case of substance addiction, a therapist may ask recovering addicts to examine their thoughts and behaviors before and after drug use. This process can identify triggers and prevent relapses (or abusing drugs again).

Recovering addicts may also seek inpatient or residential treatment programs. Inpatient treatment means that recovering addicts check into a center, where they live while undergoing detoxification and therapy. The average stay for an inpatient program is about one month. These programs offer a full-time treatment staff (such as doctors and therapists) and a very controlled environment, with few triggers. A trigger is something that comes before an action. For example, suppose that each time an alcoholic passes by the liquor store, he goes in, buys beer, and starts drinking. The liquor store is a physical trigger. There are also emotional triggers, like when an alcoholic uses drinking to deal with getting upset. Inpatient care limits an addict's exposure to triggers.

Intervention

Intervention is a way to help an addict acknowledge the addiction, see the need for change, and seek help. During this process, family members and friends share how an addict's behavior has affected them. Intervention involves helping the addict realize the pain and suffering that his or her actions have caused. The goal is to help the addict seek treatment. A trained professional called an intervention-ist leads these discussions. The role of the interventionist is to listen, provide guidance, direct the discussion, and offer treatment plans.

Interventions can be challenging when addicts are in denial, or unwilling to admit their addictions. Denial can also lead to defensive behavior, as addicts justify (rather than confront) the effects of their actions. For this reason, interventions strive to be nonjudgmental. For example, suppose that the feelings of an addict's sister were hurt when her brother stole her money to buy alcohol. Rather than accuse her brother of stealing, the sister can say, "It made me sad and angry when I saw that my money was stolen."

There are three stages to inpatient care. During the first stage, the recovering addict learns the rules and expecta-tions of the center and meets the treatment team. The addict also figures out his or her recovery needs and goals. The sec-ond phase involves the actual treatment and rehabilitation. It includes going through therapy and making positive changes that will support a life of sobriety, such as learning to take responsibility for one's actions and developing ways to cope (or deal with tough situations). During the third phase, the recovering addict reenters society. The treatment team can help by setting up outpatient therapy sessions, giving advice about schools or jobs, or suggesting a self-help group, like a twelve-step program.

Twelve-Step Programs

There are twelve-step programs that support recovering addicts. The most famous program is called Alcoholics Anonymous (AA), which is a voluntary, worldwide organization of addicts dedicated to leading sober and productive lives. This self-help program provides a safe place for recovering addicts to learn, discuss, share, cope, and move forward. It gives recovering addicts the tools to deal with cravings and triggers, while avoiding substance abuse.

The only requirement of AA is a commitment to being sober. More than two million people attend AA meetings throughout the world. These confidential meetings are an important part of the AA program, which focuses on living one day at a time. There are twelve steps to AA, which include admitting the addiction, taking responsibility for one's actions, and making amends to people who were hurt by the addiction. AA also provides recovering addicts with sponsors who provide guidance.

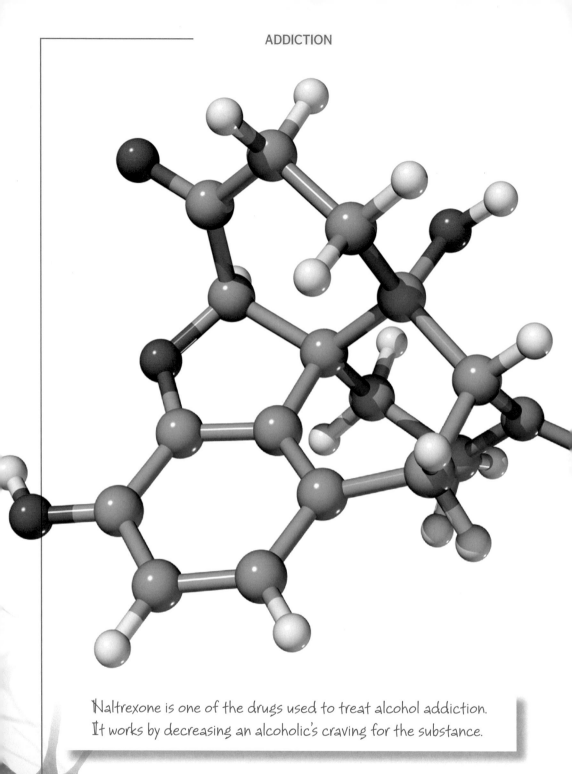

Naltrexone is one of the drugs used to treat alcohol addiction. It works by decreasing an alcoholic's craving for the substance.

Several twelve-step programs that treat addiction have been modeled after AA. These include Gamblers Anonymous (GA), Marijuana Anonymous (MA), Overeaters Anonymous (OA), and Sex Addicts Anonymous (SAA). These other programs help recovering addicts deal with their gambling, marijuana, food, and sex addictions.

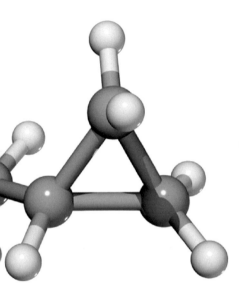

There are also twelve-step recovery programs for family members or friends of addicts, including Al-Anon and Alateen. Al-Anon provides support for families with an addict, and Alateen focuses on teens with addicts in their families.

Anti-Addiction Medications

Psychopharmacological therapy involves using medications to help recovering addicts deal with their addictions. Until recently, the medications disulfiram (Antabuse) and naltrexone were mainly used to treat addicts. Antabuse makes people feel sick to their stomachs when they consume alcohol. This deters addicts from drinking, but it has also kept many alcoholics from trying this medication.

MYTHS AND FACTS

Myth: The definition of addiction has not changed in the past twenty years.

Fact: Twenty years ago, addiction was viewed as a personality disorder or moral weakness. Today, it is seen as a chronic brain disease with effects that are measurable on imaging tests like functional MRIs.

Myth: A person who drinks a few times is not addicted to alcohol.

Fact: According to the American Psychiatric Association, a person has a substance addiction if he or she displays three or more of the following symptoms in one year: tolerance for the drug, withdrawal, loss of control, preoccupation with obtaining and using the drug, harmful consequences, and continued use despite harmful effects.

Myth: Addiction is a disease that you cannot treat.

Fact: Addiction is a chronic but treatable disease. Addiction can be treated with behavioral therapy, medicine, personal support, and a lifetime commitment to making healthy decisions.

Naltrexone decreases an addict's craving for alcohol and opiates. It needs to be taken every day. Many addicts forget or choose not to take this medication daily, though, which can result in relapses.

Today, there is a new world of anti-addiction medications, such as Vivitrol. The U.S. Food and Drug Administration (FDA) approved this medication to treat alcoholics in 2006. Vivitrol reduces the urge to drink by working on the opioid receptors for certain brain cells. Basically, the medication blocks alcohol molecules from getting to these receptors. This means that a person cannot experience the high from drugs because the pleasure pathways are blocked. An addict's cravings can actually decrease by up to 90 percent. The addict can still feel the negative effects of drug abuse, such as slurred speech. Drinking is no longer a fun activity for the addict. Vivitrol's active ingredient is naltrexone. However, Vivitrol is only taken once a month (not every day) and is given as an injection by a doctor. Both of these aspects help decrease drug abuse and increase sobriety. In October 2010, Vivitrol was approved for opioid addicts, such as heroin and morphine addicts.

The second major breakthrough came in 2004 when the FDA approved Campral to treat alcoholics. Campral actually helps the brain function properly again. It rebalances certain neurotransmitters, most likely in the GABA and glutamate systems, to heal the brain more quickly. Drinking a lot of alcohol and becoming tolerant affects the GABA and glutamate systems. Campral appears to restore their balance. By doing so, recovering addicts are more likely to remain sober by making good decisions and accepting other treatments. Both Vivitrol and Campral are themselves nonaddictive medications.

There are other medications that can also be used to treat addicts:

Name of Medication	Substance Abuse	What It Does	How It Works	FDA Approved
Topiramate (Topamax)	Alcohol	Decreases alcohol cravings and helps with withdrawal	May lower levels of dopamine in the brain	FDA-approved for treatment of seizures. Not FDA-approved for addiction.
Baclofen (Lioresal)	Alcohol/ opioid and currently being studied for cocaine abuse	Aids in withdrawal (used mostly as a muscle relaxant and antispasticity medication)	Works on GABA receptors	FDA-approved in 1977 for muscle spasms. Injection form (Gablofen) was FDA-approved in November 2010.
Suboxone	Opioid (like heroin and morphine)	Decreases the craving	Binds to opiate receptors	FDA-approved in 2002
Other antiseizure medications	Pharmaceutical sedatives and barbiturates	Decreases anxiety in a nonaddicting way	Thought to work on GABA receptors	FDA-approved

Anti-addictive medications have changed the way professionals treat addiction, which is a disease that affects millions of Americans.

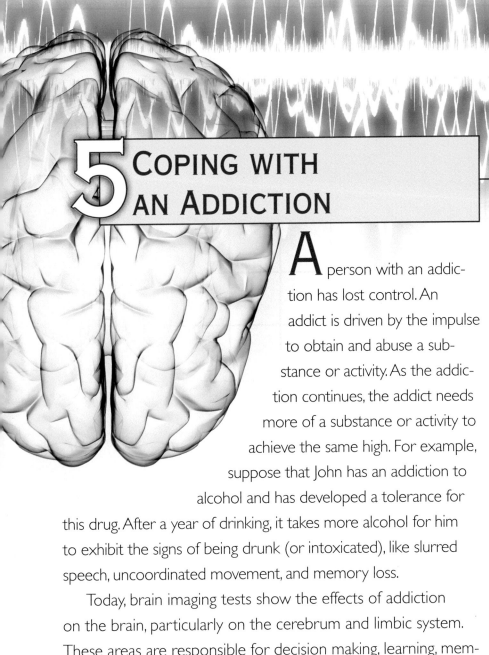

5 COPING WITH AN ADDICTION

A person with an addiction has lost control. An addict is driven by the impulse to obtain and abuse a substance or activity. As the addiction continues, the addict needs more of a substance or activity to achieve the same high. For example, suppose that John has an addiction to alcohol and has developed a tolerance for this drug. After a year of drinking, it takes more alcohol for him to exhibit the signs of being drunk (or intoxicated), like slurred speech, uncoordinated movement, and memory loss.

Today, brain imaging tests show the effects of addiction on the brain, particularly on the cerebrum and limbic system. These areas are responsible for decision making, learning, memory, and behavioral control. Substance addiction changes the brain's neurotransmitter systems, causing the brain to adapt to an addictive state. These changes make recovery more difficult,

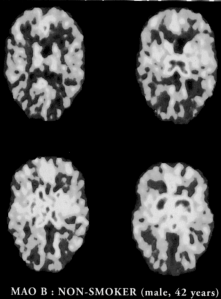

MAO B : NON-SMOKER (male, 42 years)

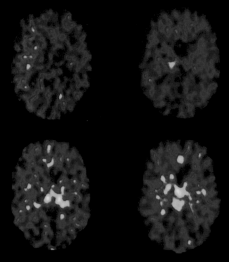

MAO B : SMOKER (male, 44 years)

This PET scan shows the brains of a non-smoker (*top*) and smoker (*bottom*). The smoker's brain has much lower levels of the enzyme MAO B, which breaks down the neurotransmitter dopamine, evidence of the addictive nature of tobacco.

since they impair parts of the brain responsible for control and effective decision making.

Managing Relapse

A relapse is a return to addictive behavior after abstaining for a period of time. Suppose that John is an alcoholic who entered an inpatient treatment program. Throughout the program, John was sober. He made the mistake of thinking that the program "cured" him. John did not realize that being sober means making healthy decisions every day. Shortly after he left the program, an old friend invited John to a party. John went to the party and was drinking again by the end of the night. John's case is not unusual. According to Harold C. Urschell III, in *Healing the Addicted Brain*, 70 to 80 percent of alcoholics relapse after finishing their treatment programs.

By viewing addiction as a personality disorder or moral weakness, people are more likely to relapse. This happens because recovering addicts view their addictions as curable with a single treatment, like a program. But by viewing addiction as a chronic and treatable brain disease, recovering addicts understand that treating addiction requires making healthy decisions, maintaining control, and accepting responsibility every single day.

Addicts may choose a twelve-step program, therapy, or anti-addictive medications to help them acquire these tools. For

Recovering Addicts and Emotional Disorders

According to Harold C. Urschell III, in *Healing the Addicted Brain*, "Over half of those with addictions also suffer from emotional or psychiatric disorders." These emotional disorders include depression (a mood disorder that involves sadness and anger), bipolar disorder (extreme mood swings), attention deficit-hyperactivity disorder (ADHD), and schizophrenia (multiple personalities). Having both an emotional disorder and an addiction (called a dual diagnosis) makes confronting substance abuse and recovery even more difficult. Effective recovery plans treat and manage both diseases.

example, suppose that John began attending AA meetings after his inpatient treatment program. When his friend invited him to the party, John wanted to go. He called his AA sponsor, who talked to him about the real possibility of a relapse if he went to the party. After this discussion, John chose not to attend the party.

Helping an Addict

Addiction affects more than just the addict himself or herself. It devastates the addict's family and friends. It can even affect complete strangers, like the victims of drunk driving accidents. Addiction can cause family members to feel anxious, embarrassed, angry, guilty, abandoned, and helpless. Their reactions to living with an addict include covering up the addict's issues, working around the addict, and trying to take on the responsibilities that addicts fail to fulfill. For example, suppose that Angela was asked to pick up her sister, Elsa, from school. But Angela got high on marijuana and forgot. Her mom left work early to pick up Elsa and made up an excuse for Angela's behavior.

There are many reasons why people become dependent on substances such as drugs and alcohol. Often, the addict must reach rock bottom to realize the severity of the problem.

Now, suppose that Angela grows up with an alcoholic father. Their home is chaotic with frequent fighting. Sometimes, her dad is very drunk, and he hits Angela and her mom. As a young child, Angela was withdrawn, confused, and had low self-esteem. She had trouble focusing in school,

Children of addicts can feel angry, worried, sad, embarrassed, hurt, and helpless. They may be victims of abuse and are at higher risk for becoming addicts themselves.

while constantly worrying about going home. Deep inside, Angela blamed herself for her dad's behavior and tried to think of ways to be "better." As a teen, Angela became depressed. She decided to try drugs herself. Shortly after, Angela joined the party scene and began dating an alcoholic. Family members (like Angela) and friends often develop poor self-esteem, depression, anxiety disorders, frequent medical issues, and even turn into addicts themselves. They can be the victims of physical and emotional abuse and possibly even sexual abuse.

Codependency is a relationship that exists between an addict and a family member or friend. The relationship may appear loving, but it is actually harmful. For example, suppose that Jason is an alcoholic and has a girlfriend named Ellen. Jason has blown all of his rent money on alcohol and needs a place to stay. Ellen offers her apartment. This help may come from a good place—her love. It can actually be harmful, though, because it enables Jason to continue his substance abuse without taking responsibility for his actions and their negative consequences. It also causes Jason to become dependent on Ellen to fix his problems, rather than encourage him to fix his own problems. Codependency can be active, like Ellen giving Jason a place to stay. It can also be passive, such as Ellen pretending not to notice when a drunken Jason stumbles into her apartment.

Support groups can help family members of addicts keep informed, acknowledge their own feelings, and develop healthy ways of coping.

Codependency is a way for family members to cope with the addict in their lives. But it is a short-term fix. It may reduce tensions and fighting in the house today. However, it also keeps the addict from acknowledging his or her actions, accepting the negative consequences, and even seeking the help needed for recovery. Codependency creates many negative feelings among the addict's family members, who often become depressed, distrustful, avoid their own feelings (because they no longer matter), and even develop stress-related diseases. As Urschel writes in his book *Healing the Addicted Brain*, "It doesn't matter if a son lives fifty miles away and only sees his addicted mother on weekends, or if a sister sees her addicted brother once a year. When an addict is part of any family arrangement, the consequences of his or her behavior will be felt by everyone."

A Lifetime Commitment

Addictions are harmful to both addicts and their family and friends. Addicts who never seek treatment or relapse can face hospitalization, organ failure, divorce, financial ruin, and even death. Addiction is a chronic, but treatable, brain disease. As with other diseases, addiction must be managed. Brain imaging tests have confirmed that addictions cause changes in the brain and that being sober can possibly heal the brain. Rehabilitation programs, twelve-step programs, and anti-addictive medications help addicts who have stopped abusing drugs. Addiction is treatable, but it requires a lifelong commitment to being sober.

Glossary

abuse The continuous use of a substance, regardless of health, social, legal, and financial costs.

addiction A chronic and treatable brain disease that involves substances and/or behavioral choices, regardless of social, health, and financial costs.

behavioral addiction Uncontrollable acts that dominate a person's time and attention.

cerebrum The thinking part of the brain that accounts for 85 percent of the brain's weight.

craving A strong desire for something.

denial An unwillingness to admit something, such as an addiction.

detoxification The process of freeing a person from addiction to an intoxicating substance.

dopamine A neurotransmitter that is responsible for making people feel pleasure.

drug experimentation The act of trying out a drug, like alcohol, marijuana, or nicotine, to see what it feels like.

GABA (gamma-aminobutyric acid) An amino acid that keeps the brain from being overexcited and allows for relaxation and sleep.

impulse control The ability to control an inclination toward an unpremeditated action.

inhibit To slow down or decrease efficacy.

intervention The process of becoming involved in order to change an addict's behavior.

limbic system The part of the brain that includes the amygdala, the hippocampus, and the hypothalamus; it is involved in emotion, motivation, and behavior.

neurotransmitter A chemical that acts as a nerve cell communicator by transmitting nerve impulses.

relapse A return to addictive behavior or recurrence of disease after abstaining for a period of time.

sobriety Abstaining (or not using) drugs.

stimulate To heighten reception or arousal of the senses.

substance addiction An addiction that involves the repeated use of drugs, such as alcohol and marijuana.

withdrawal The act of abstaining from a substance that one is addicted to and dealing with the symptoms that result from this abstinence.

For More Information

Alcoholics Anonymous

A. A. World Services, Inc.
475 Riverside Drive at West 120th Street, 11th Floor
New York, NY 10115
Web site: http://www.aa.org

This twelve-step program is for men and women dedicated to living sober.
The Web site also provides information on times and places of
meetings in the United States and Canada.

Centre for Addiction and Mental Health

250 College Street (College and Spadina)
Toronto, ON M5T 1R8
Canada
(416) 535-8501
Web site: http://www.camh.net

This is Canada's leading addiction and mental health organization.

Drug Prevention Network of Canada (DPNC)

4438 West 10th Avenue, Suite 178
Vancouver, BC V6R 4R8
Canada
Web site: http://www.dpnoc.ca

The DPNC brings together organizations and individuals dedicated to preventing, educating, and treating substance use and abuse.

Gamblers Anonymous

International Service Office

P.O. Box 17173

Los Angeles, CA 90017

(213) 386-8789

Web site: http://www.gamblersanonymous.org

This twelve-step program is for people who share the desire to stop gambling. The site also provides information on times and places of meetings.

National Association for Children of Alcoholics

10920 Connecticut Avenue, Suite 100

Kensington, MD 20895

(888) 55-4COAS [2627] or (301)468-0985

Web site: http://www.nacoa.org

This organization provides information, such as where to get help, for children of parents with drug addictions.

National Institute on Alcohol Abuse and Alcoholism (NIAAA)

5635 Fishers Lane

Bethesda, MD 20892

(301) 443-3860

Web site: http://www.niaaa.nih.gov

The NIAAA is involved in national efforts to decrease alcohol-related problems in many ways, such as researching prevention, treatment, genetics, and health risks.

National Institutes of Health

6001 Executive Boulevard, Room 5213

Bethesda, MD 20892-9561

(301) 443-1124

Web site: http://www.nida.nih.gov

This organization conducts research that improves prevention, treatment, and policy concerning drug addictions.

Web Sites

Due to the changing nature of Internet links, Rosen Publishing has developed an online list of Web sites related to the subject of this book. This site is updated regularly. Please use this link to access the list:

http://www.rosenlinks.com/bdis/add

For Further Reading

Curry, Constance, and Kristina Wandzilak. *The Lost Years: Surviving a Mother and Daughter's Worst Nightmare.* Santa Monica, CA: Jeffers Press, 2006.

Franklin, Karen, and Lauren King. *Addicted Like Me: A Mother-Daughter Story of Substance Abuse and Recovery.* Berkley, CA: Seal Press, 2009.

Herzanek, Joe. *Why Don't They Just Quit?* Boulder, CO: Changing Lives Foundation, 2010.

McCown, William G., and William A. Howatt. *Treating Gambling Problems.* Hoboken, NJ: John Wiley and Sons, 2007.

Morrone, Lisa. *Overcoming Overeating: It's Not What You Eat, It's What's Eating You.* Eugene, OR: Harvest House Publishers, 2009.

Moyers, William Cope. *Broken.* New York, NY: Penguin, 2007.

Nabuco de Abreu, Cristiano, and Kimberley S. Young. *Internet Addiction: A Handbook and Guide to Evaluation and Treatment.* Hoboken, NJ: John Wiley and Sons, 2011.

Najavits, Lisa M. *A Woman's Addiction Workbook: Your Guide to In-Depth Healing.* Oakland, CA: New Harbinger Publications, 2007.

Palaian, Sally. *Spent: Break the Buying Obsession and Discover Your True Worth.* Center City, MN: Hazelden Publishing, 2009.

Peele, Stanton. *Addiction Proof Your Child: A Realistic Approach to Preventing Drug, Alcohol, and Other Dependencies.* New York, NY: Three Rivers Press, 2007.

Roberts, Kevin. *Cyber Junkie: Escape the Gaming and Internet Trap.* Center City, MN: Hazelden Publishing, 2010.

Robinson, Bryan. *Chained to the Desk: A Guidebook for Workaholics, Their Partners and Children, and the Clinicians Who Treat Them.* New York, NY: New York University Press, 2007.

Sheff, David. *Beautiful Boy.* New York, NY: Harcourt, 2008.

Sheff, Nic. *Tweak.* New York, NY: Atheneum, 2009.

Index

About the Author

Barbara Gottfried Hollander has worked in many areas of education as a curriculum developer, course writer, classroom teacher, and private learning consultant in both mainstream and special education schools. She has authored numerous books for teens, including *Paying for College: Practical, Creative Strategies*. Hollander received a B.A. in economics from the University of Michigan and an M.A. in economics from New York University.

Photo Credits

Cover (brain), pp. 8, 10, 14, 24, 27, 30–31 Shutterstock; p. 12 Carol & Mike Werner/Visuals Unlimited, Inc./Getty Images; p. 17 Kallista Images/Getty Images; p. 19 Yoray Liberman/Getty Images News/ Getty Images; p. 21 Universal Images Group/Diverse Images/ Getty Images; p. 32 istockphoto/Thinkstock; p. 36 © Spencer Grant/PhotoEdit; pp. 40–41 Laguna Design/Photo Researchers; p. 46 Pascal Goetgheluck/Photo Researchers; p. 49 © www. istockphoto.com/DIMUSE; p. 50 © www.istockphoto.com/Chris Price; pp. 52–53 © Mary Kate Denny/PhotoEdit; cover, back cover, and interior background images and elements (nerve cells, brain waves, brains) Shutterstock.com.

Designer: Les Kanturek; Editor: Nicholas Croce; Photo Researcher: Marty Levick